Think Outside the Box

*21 Days to
A Clear Direction*

By Prophetess Sebe Dalieh

Think Outside the Box: 21 Days to A Clear Direction
Published by Leading Through Living Community LLC

Copyright 2016 by Sebe Dalieh

ISBN-10: 0-9983482-2-8
ISBN-13: 978-0-9983482-2-3

Editing by and Cover design by Lynita Mitchell-Blackwell

Scripture quotations are from the Holy Bible, King James Version (KJV) - www.Bible.com

All Rights Reserved. No part or portion of this publication may be reproduced, stored in a retrieval system, or transmitted in any form or by any means - electronic, mechanical, photocopying, recording, or otherwise - without the express written consent of the author.

For information:
Leading Through Living Community LLC
6790 W. Broad Street Suite 300
Douglasville, GA 30134

Dedication

This book is dedicated to all of my supporters and my three sons: Mark, Jr., Matthew, and Mel.

Acknowledgement

I acknowledge the Holy Spirit who continues to lead and guide me. I want to celebrate all of my divine connections and say, thank you! Thanks for propelling me into purpose.

Foreword

If you should ever find yourself discouraged, out of touch with the Lord, or troubled by the uncertainties of life, I pray that you stop trying everything else and take time to read this guide to finding clarity. Consider turning unto our Lord Jesus Christ, the Master of all things.

St. John 14:27, *"Peace I leave with you, my peace I give unto you: not as the world giveth, give I unto you. Let not your heart be troubled, neither let it be afraid."*

Introduction:
Why We Need Direction

Today, there are too many spiritually weak people living beneath their God-given potential. They are isolated, frustrated, depressed, angry, restless, discouraged, half-happy, half-fulfilled, and confused. Many are wondering if they will ever get to live the abundant life that Christ promised. They are seeking Godly direction and honestly want to do the right thing. However in their pursuit of finding God, they endure so many missed steps that place them out of balance, leaving them too far left or too far right - from one extreme to the other. They do too much of one thing and not enough of everything. These poor souls either spend too much time praying without believing, or they have an enormous amount of faith, but take no action. They run from place to place seeking insight and guidance, looking to man instead of seeking insight from God.

Some people say they have prayed, yet have received no answers as to what to do, leaving them even more hopeless, despondent, isolated, confused, anxious and frustrated about life.

With so many choices available in this "anything goes" society, many people find themselves falling, making one mistake after another, putting their confidence and trust in people instead of God. After feeling as though they have tried everything, their mind swirls with more questions than answers. They begin to ask themselves the same questions:

"What should I do?"

"What do I do when I don't know what to do?"

Many people ask:

"What should I do?"

"What do I do when I don't know what to do?"

The answer is simple and should always be: SEEK GOD!

God can give you a thought or knowledge that is so outside the box that you know beyond a shadow of a doubt that it came from Him.

GOD CAN MAKE YOU THINK OUTSIDE THE BOX.

Because everything we do stems from our limited understanding, we end up making a ton of mistakes. God can keep you in line. He wants to give you ideas, wisdom, thoughts, knowledge, understanding and direction that are way beyond your capacity. Study God's word, get to know Him, and let Him guide you and give you life. It is when you do not operate within the template of God's word that setbacks and ultimate destruction occur.

God wants to give you ideas, wisdom, thoughts, knowledge, understanding and direction that are far beyond your capacity.

Hosea 4:6 states, *"My people are destroyed for the lack of knowledge: because thou hast rejected knowledge, I will also reject thee..."*

So what does this have to do with thinking outside of the box?

Well, let us first examine what it means to "Think outside the Box!"

Time

Often times, when we have come to the very end of ourselves, it is the same time that God can begin to work on our behalf. God is not on our timetable, therefore He is not bound by time. God owns time itself. God is not bound by nature, therefore Mother Nature has nothing on Him.

My Bible tells me that God has a set time, the right time, the appointed time, and He works at His appointed time in due season. According to Romans 5:6, *"For when we were yet without strength, in due time Christ died for the ungodly."* (Emphasis added.)

That means before the creation of time, God was thinking about you. Before you ever ran into your "situation", God had you on His mind. Before you tried to figure out a solution, God had a plan in place. Before you were formed, God was at work!

GOD IS, GOD WAS, and GOD WILL FOREVER BE!

Jeremiah 1:5 states, *"Before I formed thee in the belly I knew thee; and before thou camest forth out of the womb I sanctified thee, and I ordained thee a prophet unto the nations."*

Before the creation of time, God was thinking about you.

Knowing

God had you all figured out. He knew all about the struggles you were going to face. God already knew the situations that would try your patience and your faith, yet He allowed them because He called and ordained you for such times as these.

Yes, the struggles and inconsistences of life can be trying, but you are built and wired to face them.

There are so many struggles in life, however, the greatest of these is the struggle of confusion. Simply not knowing what to do.

What do you do when you just don't know what to do? The word of God has clear instructions on what to do when a person has no idea as to what must be done to accomplish his/her goals.

You are uniquely built and wired to face life's struggles and inconsistences.

In this book, I will walk you through the Word to gain a better understanding of God's methodologies. This understanding will allow you to think outside the box, as God gives you a clear direction for the situations you may face in life.

To think outside the box simply means thinking outside of "Self."

It means to think of everything you are capable of doing outside your own strength or power. It means getting out of the "woe is me mentality". It means getting rid of the "poor me" mentality - that defeated mindset that magnifies all of your problems, flaws, failures, insecurities, weaknesses, mishaps, and issues that leave you thinking as a victim of circumstance.

To think outside the box simply means thinking outside of "Self."

The "woe is me" and "poor me" mentalities put you in a defeated state of mind, leaving you convinced that there is no way your situation can change.

Let us consider two passages of scripture. These scriptures will show you that God will make things clear to you. They will also teach you to trust God in your time of need, confusion and distress.

"After these things the word of the Lord came unto Abram in a vision, saying, Fear not, Abram: I am thy shield, and thy exceeding great reward. And Abram said, Lord GOD what wilt thou give me, seeing I go childless, and the steward of my house is this Eliezer of Damascus? And Abram said, Behold, to me thou hast given no seed; and, lo, one born in my house is mine heir." Genesis 15:1-3

Here in these verses, we see that Abram receives a vision from God. In this vision, God tells him, 'Do not fear, I am your protector, I am your joy.'

But as you can see, Abram is concerned about many things. He cannot fully believe that God will bless him with his heart's desire. Abram had a "double mind": he believed God, believed that God is God, and believed God to be the most high… yet there was something on Abram's mind that he really wanted, and he was not sure or confident that God was going to do it for him.

Abram wanted a child. He and his wife were old, well stricken in years and had not been able to conceive. Abram believed God to make him a father of many nations, but he did not quite believe that this nation would stem from his own loins.

"And, behold, the word of the Lord came unto him, saying, 'This shall not be thine heir; but he that shall come forth out of thine own bowels shall be thine heir.'" Genesis 15:4

God is so faithful.

If you noticed, God had to speak to Abram to make sure that Abram understood "His" vision. God wanted Abram to rest in Him. He made it clear to Abram that his obedience unto Him was not in vain. God was going to reward Abram.

As humans we feel burdened. Oftentimes we become weary, worried, anxious, fearful, and are sometimes attacked by the enemy with an illness – these afflictions leave us uncertain as to God's intentions. We begin to wonder if God will be there for us. We ask ourselves, "Can God or will God help me?"

God is faithful.

The answer to these questions is, "YES!"

And

"I know God can."

And

"I know He is able."

It is the lack of faith that leads some to then wonder, "But will He do it for me?"

You are not alone in the struggle. Even Abram struggled, and *he* later became Abraham the "father of nations"! Abraham is a prime example of how strong our faith should be. He initially struggled to fully trust God's word:

- He took Lot, his brother's son, with him when he was instructed to leave his country,

- Abram lied and said Sari was his sister, instead of his wife when confronted by foreign spies, and
- He wondered if God would do for him the one thing that he really wanted - a child.

Even with all of what God said unto Abram in the vision, he still listened to his wife, Sari and tried to bring about the promise from his own understanding through his maid Hagar. With all of that, God still knew Abram was true in his heart, and had the faith of a mustard seed. God knew that Abram was limited in his understanding. Yet God still blessed him and fulfilled His promise unto him. Abraham was exceedingly blessed, as he became the father of many nations and an example of our faith should be in Christ – truly a Faith "Hall of Fame" inductee!

It's clearly not by our works but by God's grace. Amen.

Let us take a look at our second passage of scripture:

"Then there came some that told Jehoshaphat, saying, 'There cometh a great multitude against thee from beyond the sea on this side Syria; and behold, they be in Hazazontamar which is Engedi.' And Jehoshaphat feared, and set himself to seek the Lord, and proclaimed a fast throughout all Judah." II Chronicles 20:2-3

King Jehoshaphat was a godly king (one after God's own heart), but that did not stop the adversary from attacking him. Nations rose up against him to bring him down. The Bible says, King Jehoshaphat 'feared greatly.' He was terrified and faced enormous pressure.

Even those who live their lives according to God's own heart must deal with attacks from the adversary.

The Bible says there were some good found in the king. He prepared his heart to seek the Lord. But what did this king <u>not</u> do? He did not:

- Call his other colleagues to talk about his troubles
- Sit around worrying about his troubles
- Snap ill-advised orders at his army or advisers
- Call the prophet to hear what God had to say.

King Jehoshaphat <u>got on his knees</u> and <u>inquired of the Lord</u> for himself. He set himself and the nation at large to seek the Lord.

Friend, I do not know what trials you are facing right now. You may be dealing with depression, oppression, worry, tremendous pressure, disappointment, illness, loss of a loved one, loss of income, rejection, defeat, confusion or diverse temptations. I believe you should set your heart and mind to seek God. Stop thinking about yourself and how big your problems are, and think about all of what God has done for you, and how big your God is!

Yes, I know it is hard to think of what to do when faced with real troubles that are visible. Yet, sometimes the very thing that you think is working against you, can actually be working for you. And the only way to know that is by seeking God's holy counsel.

Think outside the box. The box represents you. Think outside of yourself. Open your mind to receive the teachings of God. Allow that ancient and all-knowing wisdom inside your mind. Allow it to transform you and renew your strength.

Set your heart and mind to seek God.

You are God's workmanship, to be utilized for His purpose. Life is not all about you. Life is about bringing glory to God. When we are blessed by our work, it is simply a wonderful byproduct of our obedience and faithfulness.

Oftentimes when faced with pressure, difficulties or disappointments, the very first thing that comes to our mind is,

"How is this going to affect Me?"

Then followed by,

"How will I appear to others?"

And then,

"What will people say or think of me?"

We get so consumed with self and others' thoughts and feelings that we do not stop to think about God's glory nor His grace. We cannot visualize the possibilities and meaning of our struggles. We fail to realize how our struggles may help us spiritually mature.

Realize that not everything bad that happens to you is meant for bad! I know, that is quite a revelation! And someone is going to receive it and be blessed by it.

Sometimes when unfortunate situations occur, these situations may be the very thing that God uses to grow or elevate you.

Joseph said it perfectly in Genesis 50:20:
"Fear not: for am I in the place of God? But as for you, ye thought evil against me; but God meant it for good, to bring to pass, as it is this day to save much people alive."

God wants to give you an eternal knowledge, the kind of knowledge that will make you better comprehend your situation.

Some disappointments can become reappointments to accelerate you and bring God glory. So when you are going through your struggle, do not call another person on the phone whining or grinding about your situation.

Do not get on the internet to get answers from Google search. Do not even read another motivational book. Oops! {About to put myself out of business}
Think outside the box and seek God's infinite wisdom.

Call on the Lord, and ask Him. "Lord, what does this mean?" God has all the answers.

Psalm 34:4 says, "I sought the Lord, and He heard me, and delivered me from all my fears."

God wants to give you an eternal knowledge, the kind of knowledge that will make you better comprehend your situation. The kind of knowledge that will make you understand that it could not have been done by any other means except by the hand of God.

King Jehoshaphat was a great king. The Bible says that the Lord established him because he walked in the ways of the Lord. The King knew that he could not rule the great nation of Israel without the knowledge and wisdom of God. Therefore, he thought outside the box to seek God. This great king's heart was lifted up in the ways of the Lord. He sought the Lord and he received divine answers.

In 2 Chronicles 20:14-17, The word of the Lord came to the prophet Jahaziel in the midst of the congregation while they were yet praying and said, *"Hearken ye, all Judah, and ye inhabitants of Jerusalem, and thou king*

Jehoshaphat, Thus saith the Lord unto you, Be not afraid nor dismayed by reason of this great multitude; for the battle is not yours, but God's."

Here was this great king's answer from the living God! O yes, you can put a stamp on it – the message will be delivered. You can write a check on it – knowing that it is good and will clear the bank!

The king thought outside the box and sought the Lord and that is when he received real answers.

When God speaks His word, it settles any situation no matter how long it takes. All of God's words end in, "Yes" and "Amen." When God says it is finished, it is finished! Period! You may not see it, or even feel it in the natural, but believe me, it is finished. All you need to do is believe it, receive it, say thank the Lord, and walk in your conviction.

What are you dealing with that caused your blindness in believing God's word? Are you ready for deliverance?

Let us prepare to be delivered and set free:

Follow the instructions.

Follow the instructions.

FOLLOW THE INSTRUCTIONS.

King Jehoshaphat followed God's instructions. He was obedient. The first thing he did after he got his breakthrough was worship the ever-living God.

Oftentimes when we receive a word from God, we forget to give Him thanks, and we forget to continue in our worship and praise unto

Him. We forget to stay in adoration unto Him.

That was the exact situation with the ten lepers in Luke 17. After the lepers asked for healing from Jesus and Jesus had mercy upon them as they were cleansed. Nine of them went about their business, they forgot to give thanks while only one returned to Jesus to thank Him and Jesus made him whole.

Luke 17:11-17
"And it came to pass, as he went to Jerusalem, that he passed through the midst of Samaria and Galilee. And as he entered into a certain village, there met him ten men that were lepers, which stood afar off: And they lifted up their voices, and said, Jesus, Master, have mercy on us.
And when he saw them, he said unto them, Go shew yourselves unto the priests. And it came to pass, that, as they went, they were cleansed. And one of them, when

he saw that he was healed, turned back and with a loud voice glorified God, and fell down on his face at his feet, giving him thanks: and he was a Samaritan. And Jesus answering said, were there not ten cleansed? But where are the nine?"

We are victorious by the word of the Lord!

But King Jehoshaphat did not forget. He knew he was victorious by the word of the Lord and he knew God had kept His promises. Therefore, we read in 2 Chronicles 20:18-19, "And Jehoshaphat bowed his head with his face to the ground: and all Judah and the inhabitants of Jerusalem fell before the Lord, worshipping the Lord. And the Levites, of the children of the Kohathites, and children of the Korhited, stood up to praise the Lord God of Israel with a loud voice on high."

The king offered thanks and praises unto the Lord because he knew no one else could have helped him in his situation but God. The Lord gave him peace and fought for him.

Sometimes God will allow things to happen to you and for you that you did not think about or ever have imagined, and you know in your spirit that no one else other than the Lord could have made it happened. It was all by the hand and grace of God.

After King Jehoshaphat gave thanks, and offered worship and praises unto God, he became obedient. This is a critical point because no amount of praise and worship can erase a disobedient spirit. God expects His servants to be obedient to His instructions.

The King then rose up early the next morning, and went forth into the wilderness of Tekoa and said, *"Hear me, O Judah, and ye inhabitants of Jerusalem; Believe in the Lord your God so shall ye be established; believe his prophets, so shall ye prosper. And when he had consulted with the people, he appointed singers unto the Lord, and that should praise the beauty of holiness, as they went out before the army, and to say, Praise the*

Lord; for his mercy endureth forever." 2 Chronicles 20:20-21

The King called upon his faith, obedience, worship, praise, and thanks unto God to face his enemy. And the Bible says as they sang praises unto the Lord, the Lord set ambushes (II Chronicles 20:22- English Standard Version) against their enemies, and their enemies were smitten as they utterly slay and destroy themselves.

All Judah did was watch; they did not have to fight this battle. As the children of Judah watched, their enemies fought amongst themselves and behold they saw a great multitude of dead bodies.

When the fighting was over, King Jehoshaphat, all of Judah, and the inhabitants of Jerusalem took an enormous amount of precious jewels for themselves, the sum of which they could not carry away in one day. In fact, it took them three days to gather and cart away the spoils.

The King and his people assembled themselves in the Valley of Berachah to bless the Lord and give thanks unto God for all He had done for them. They then returned to the house of the Lord, every man unto God's house with joy, for the Lord had made them rejoice over their enemies.

"And they came to Jerusalem with psalteries and harps and trumpets unto the house of the Lord. And the fear of God was upon all the kingdoms of those countries after hearing of the fight against the enemies of Israel. So the realm of Jehoshaphat was quiet; for his God gave him rest round about."
2 Chronicles 20:28-30.

God can give you rest for your weary soul.

God can give you rest for your weary soul. He can give you peace for your anxious heart. He can put the fear of God in your enemies so that they are afraid to mess with you. But only God can do these things.

He can give you the confidence needed to be still and let Him fight for you. But you must be obedient to His word. You cannot continue to do what *you* want to do and prosper. You must listen to God, trust God, and obey God so shall He establish you and make you prosperous in all your ways.

Days To A Clear Direction

In order to get a clear direction, you first need to follow God's instructions. That sounds very simple, yet sometimes we fail to do so. Taking matters into your own hands can cause you to fail and continue in your own struggles. That's called stress. Doing with God and following His instructions is called grace where much more is accomplished effortlessly.

You cannot continue to do what you want to do and prosper. You must listen to God, trust God, and obey God.

One prime Bible example of this is King Saul. He was an ordinary man going about his own business. In fact, the Bible tells us that he was on his way to look for his father's asses when he met Samuel, God's Seer. (1 Samuel 9). Saul was clearly chosen, and anointed by God. All he had to do was obey God's instructions. Yet he chose to disobey God's commands.

In 1 Samuel 10-13, Saul was instructed by the prophet Samuel to tarry in Gilgal seven days until the prophet arrive to make offerings unto the Lord. The Bible says Saul did tarry seven days, but he did not come to Gilgal until *after* the seven days had passed. Saul took it upon himself to make the offerings unto the Lord, and as soon as he did and came to the end of it, Samuel arrived.

Samuel was displeased and asked him, "What hast thou done?" Saul began to make excuses for his unrighteous acts, but Samuel said, "[Because] thou hast not obeyed God's command therefore thou kingdom shalt not be established."

Not staying in alignment with God's word or following His instructions can cause you an enormous amount of emotional pain and grief.

Our God is a wise God. He knows all about our struggles, our insecurities, our impatience, and our hearts' desires. He knows our shortcomings and He is willing to put us back on the right track in spite of them.

O child of God, what are you dealing with that keeps you up at night? God knows that you go to bed with it on your mind and you wake up with it on your mind. Jehovah knows. Sometimes we waste so much time worrying and trying to analyze everything that it leaves us exhausted and depleted.

Take notice of what King Jehoshaphat did when he was at a cross road: he commanded himself and his people to seek God. You too can cut right to the chase and go directly to the Lord in prayer.

I pray about everything, but sometimes I become tense and cannot figure out some things and just cannot seem to put my finger on it. In those times, I become like King Jehoshaphat: I stop, drop and call on the Lord! That sounds so good!

Stop, drop and call.

Stop, drop and pray!

I think I will use this slogan quite often. When I am in trouble, who do I call? I call on the Lord!

I stop the busy-ness, overthinking, stressing, worrying, fretting, tossing and turning. I drop on the floor in my prayer closet and call on the name of the Lord.

Remember the familiar scripture, Jeremiah 29:13? It says, "And ye shall seek me, and find me when ye shall search for me with all your heart." One reason why our prayers go unanswered is because we only partially believe. When you stop depending on your human wisdom, stop depending on people, stop fearing the unknown and submit yourself unto God, valuable things happen! By valuable, I mean unexpected, supernatural.

When you surrender unto God, He comes closer to you and starts to speak to you. "Draw nigh to God and he will draw nigh unto you." James 4:8.

King Jehoshaphat received valuable instructions from God, and this time his victory was to be effortless. My, my! The Lord's response was, *"Tomorrow go ye down against them, your enemies. Ye shall find them in the wilderness of Jeruel. Ye shall not need to fight in this battle: set yourselves, stand ye still, and see the salvation of the Lord with you, O Judah and Jerusalem: fear not, nor be dismayed; tomorrow go out against them: for the Lord will be with you."*

Effortless! God was so gracious unto the King. He knew the king's heart, his weaknesses, shortcomings, and past failures and yet God looked beyond the man and led him to the path of victory. My Bible tells me that God is no respecter of persons. Acts 10:34.

What He did for the king, He can surely do the same for you.

You may very well be fighting a fight that was never meant for you to enter into, and this could be the cause of your disgust. Here is a bit of advice: cease striving and take another look. Reconsider, reevaluate, and reassess your entire situation. Do you think your situation is God's best for you? If you do not know, why don't you ask Him in prayer? He has answers that will blow your mind. You may not be ready for the answer, but you will have it if you ask the question.

Knowledge is power. What you know cannot destroy you, it is what you do not know that will destroy you. This is why God wants to keep you informed. He wants His people aware and fully knowledgeable about life. Therefore, if you want to succeed in a godly way in this life, you will keep His word in your heart. "My people are destroyed for the lack of knowledge: because thou hast rejected knowledge, I will also reject thee." Hosea 4:6

It is unlike God to leave His people uninformed. The exception is if it was part of His plan for a particular reason. God is light and those that walk with God walk in the light. They that walk in light may stumble, but they do not fall. 2 Peter says, "But grow in grace, and in the knowledge of our Lord and Savior Jesus Christ. To him be glory both now and forever. Amen."

God does not like to see His children taken advantage of by the ungodly. Therefore, He wants us to know His word. God does not want His children to be ignorant in any way, shape or form to the enemy's devices, schemes, nor tactics. 2 Corinthians 2:11 says, "Lest Satan should get an advantage of us: for we are not ignorant of his devices."

Here is one of my favorite Bible verses. I always get happy when I hear this verse!

"Now thanks be unto God, which always causeth us to triumph in Christ, and maketh manifest the savour of his knowledge by us in every place." 2 Corinthians 2:14

God makes us win in every situation. He opens our spiritual eyes, He increases our understanding, and He downloads knowledge into our spirit so that we are fully informed and aware of our surroundings.

I truly embrace the truth that God keeps His beloved informed. If I see a servant of God fallen, I know without a doubt that servant of God was not paying attention or was walking in disobedience. God keeps us informed, and He keeps us ten steps ahead of the evil one.

Need convincing? Here is a prime example of how God will look out for His faithful servants. In 1 Kings 14:4- 6 it states, "And Jeroboam's wife did so, and arose, and went to Shiloh, and came to the house of Ahijah. But Ahijah could not see; for his eyes were set by reason of his age. And the Lord said unto Ahijah, Behold, the wife of Jeroboam cometh to ask a thing of thee for her son; for he is sick: thus and thus shalt thou say unto her: for it shall be, when she cometh in, that she shall feign herself to be another woman. And it was so, when Ahijah heard the sound of her feet, as she came in at the door, that he said, Come in, thou wife of Jeroboam; why feignest thou thysely to be another?"

God is saying, "Try me! Will somebody try me? I have plenty of resources and plenty of ministering angels sitting unemployed ready to be put to work for you!"

God is on the look out for His people and He is determined to give His faithful insight in every situation. In as much as the prophet Ahijah was old and could barely see, he still could not be fooled by Jeroboam's wife's disguised. God exposed her through the prophet's spiritual eyes.

How much more will God not do for you to put you on the right track and give you a clear direction?

Beloved, God is saying, "Try me! Will somebody try me? I have plenty of resources and plenty of ministering angels sitting unemployed ready to be put to work for you!"

God wants and is willing to give you a clear direction. If you are sitting on the side lines of life, this book will help you get a clear direction and get you going in God's way.

21 Days to A Clear Direction

Why 21 Days?

It took 21 days for the man of God, Daniel, whose name was Belteshazzar to get his response from God. He did a three week focused prayer unto the Lord and received a visitation after his time of prayer and fasting. Notice, the Bible says from the first day that Daniel began to pray, his prayer was answered, but the prince of the kingdom of Persia withstood the angel. Archangel Michael fought against the prince of Persia to bring Daniel's answer. With Bible knowledge, I will help and guide you into a consistent day-to-day focused prayer that will become a way of life for you. I truly believe that if you desire change and a clear direction, you will seek God earnestly through prayer, fasting and His word. With this commitment, even before the 21-day is over, you will receive your breakthrough!

It is not rocket science, it is a principle of God's word. Some things only come through prayer and fasting.

"This kind can come forth by nothing, but by prayer and fasting." Mark 9:29

Remember, God is not bound by your time, He's bound to His word. Psalm 89:34 "My covenant will I not break, nor alter the thing that is gone out of my lips."
2 Chronicle 7:14, "If my people, which are called by my name, shall

humble themselves, and pray, and seek my face, and turn from their wicked ways; then will I hear from heaven, and will forgive their sin, and will heal their land."

Therefore, if you go before God with a humble and sincere heart, a broken and contrite spirit, the Lord will not despise you, and you will receive your healing and breakthrough.

If you go before God with a sincere heart, the Lord will not despise you, and you will receive your healing.

Before you start your 21 days of healing and deliverance, I want you to consider a few things:

1. First, get your mind, spirit and soul on one accord. Prepare yourself, Let God know that you need Him. Let Him know that you have tried everything yet and still you feel broken, anxious, worried, unfulfilled, fearful, impatient, ill in your body, ill in your mind, depressed, and/or bound by your adversities. Let Him know that you have tried everything, yet and still are insecure, still struggling with guilt, un-forgiveness, pride, low self-esteem, feeling less than, rejected, under-appreciated, under-estimated, forgotten, unworthy, unwanted… and you can add to the list whatever your issues are. God is ready to

help you walk through it and get you delivered from it all.

2. Second, choose a set time, a specific time that will allow you to be focused so that you are not disturbed or distracted. Daniel was a man of prayer. The Bible says that he had an excellent spirit. "Three times a day he got down on his knees and prayed, giving thanks before his God". Daniel 6:10.

3. The third thing that I ask is that you pray the prayer of confession. Sometimes, the trouble in our lives is self-inflicted, caused by our own disobedience and unforgiveness.

"And I prayed unto the Lord my God, and made my confession, and said, O Lord, the great and dreadful God, keeping the covenant and mercy to them that love him, and to them that keep his commandments; we have sinned, and committed iniquity, and have done wickedly, and have rebelled, even by departing from thy precepts and from thy judgments: neither have we hearkened unto thy servants the prophets. Which spake in thy name to our kings. Our princes, and our fathers and to all the people of the land." Daniel 9:4-6

I would also suggest that during these 21 days, you allow the Lord to choose a fast for you as you pray and read His word.

Let's begin!

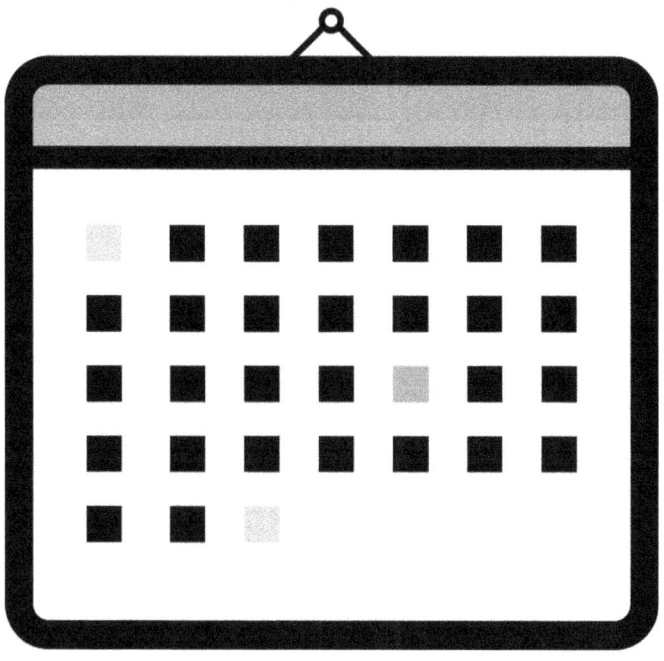

Day 1

Day 1

Read Psalm 51. Pray the prayer of confession. Ask God to forgive you of your sins.

As Christians, we need to be on high alert for sins in our lives, for they can hinder our prayers, and lead us to attacks, chastisement, misery and even death.

Sometimes we have sinned against God without even knowing it. That is called the sin of omission. In other words, we sin by not doing what we ought to be doing.

Pray to God to forgive you for the things you have intentionally done. This is called the sin of commission. This type of sin also occurs when you purposefully fail to do something you should.

Sin is sin. Yet God is faithful and merciful. With a repentant spirit, He will heal you.

Day 1 Focus Prayer

Have mercy upon me, O Lord, forgive me of my sins according to your truth and loving kindness. Wash me clean and cleanse me of my sins. I have sinned against you in so many ways, knowingly and unknowingly. I am aware that I need your total healing. I have nowhere to go and no one to go to. Therefore, I have come to you with a broken spirit and a contrite heart. I want to be free from my bondage. Hide not your face from me, create in me a clean heart, O God; and renew a right spirit within me.

Cast me not away from your presence; and take not your holy spirit away from me. Restore the joy of your salvation; and uphold me with thy free spirit. In Jesus' name. Amen.

Go to a quiet place and meditate or think about what you have just read and said. You can lie down, but remember to stay quiet and allow God to speak.

God speaks in many ways. He may whisper in your ear, speak to you in a dream or vision. *"For God speaketh once, yea twice, yet man perceiveth not. In a dream, in a vision of the night, when deep sleep falleth upon men, and sealeth their instruction, that he may withdraw man from his purpose and hide pride from man."* Job 33:14-16

God does speak and will speak to you. So do not worry if you fall asleep. He can also speak in a dream or vision but all in all, He will make you aware that it is He

who is speaking to you. You will not miss His word.
Notice that He also wants you to know that He is speaking to you. Therefore He will get your attention. Just be still, do not be anxious. He will speak to you, just read His word, pray, and be quiet as you listen for His voice.

Take note: the devil is crafty and cunning, and he also tries to speak to you through dreams. During the time of focused prayer, the enemy is even craftier and cunning as he tries to get in the way. Do not fret, all you need to know is that when God speaks, His words will line up with His holy scripture. If it is evil, it is not God.

Think Outside the Box: 21 Days to A Clear Direction
Prophetess Sebe Dalieh

Day

2

Day 2

Read Philippians 4 and pray for the peace of God.

Oftentimes the noise and distractions of this world separate us from the peace of God. We become overly concerned about many things and before long, our joy is gone. We are robbed of our peace in God.

Make your supplications known unto the Lord with thanksgiving. You may not feel like thanking God in advance, but it is the proper posture to be in before God. He is Almighty, He is all knowing and He is all powerful. Thank Him. When you thank God for your situation, you are showing Him that you trust Him to work on your behalf.

As a child of God you are instructed to rejoice in the Lord, always and in all ways. Let your moderation be known that the Lord is at hand or near. Your gentleness will show the enemy that God is with you.

God's people walk in peace at all times. They are always smiling because they know who is in control. They walk in total confidence because in every situation God is working for their good.

Day 2 Focus Prayer

O Lord, God, I surrender myself unto You. I exchange my anxiety, fear, worry and doubt for your peace. I will be careful for nothing because I am choosing to trust you, O Lord.

Make your requests, and pray not for your will but for the Lord's will to be done. The Lord knows what is best for you, in Jesus' name.

Go to a quiet place. Meditate on what you have just read and ask God to speak to you.

Day 3

Day 3

Read Psalm 138:8, and pray the prayer of assurance. *"The Lord will perfect that which concerneth me; thy mercy, O Lord, endureth forever: forsake not the works of thine own hands."*

Do you believe that God wants to perfect everything that concerns you? He does. God desires His children to be whole. That means He does not want you pre-occupied with cares when you diligently seek Him.

Too many believers go to Church, pray, read the Word and still have no faith in what God has proclaimed. How do I know? If you are anxious, worried, fearful, overly concerned about many things, and in doubt, you are walking not only in unbelief but in disobedience as well because the Word says

"Fear not"
"Be anxious for nothing"

and

"Only believe"

If you put these principles into practice, you will not only walk in victory, you will also walk in wholeness, i.e., there will be nothing lacking and nothing broken.

<u>Day 3 Focus Prayer</u>

Dear Lord Jesus, You have proclaimed unto me to walk by faith and not by sight because you are perfecting the things that concern me. I give you the honor and the glory. I will praise you with my whole heart, I will sing praises unto you, I will worship you in your holy temple because you are perfecting the things that concern me. I will settle myself in you because you are working things out for my good. I bless you and I praise your holy name. In Jesus' name. Amen.

Go to your quiet place meditate on what you read and ask God to speak to you.

Think Outside the Box: 21 Days to A Clear Direction
Prophetess Sebe Dalieh

Day 4

Day 4

Read Psalm 25. Pray for direction. With all of the noises of this world, getting divine direction can be difficult. You have to be able to distinguish God's voice from the devil's voice. As I stated earlier, if it does not align with the Word of God, it is not God. God's Word gives light to your path and peace for the situation. The scripture says, *"Thy word is a lamp unto my feet, and a light unto my path."* Psalm 119:105.

Clearly, seeking God through His Word gives us direction. Keep in mind that God is not limited, nor restricted, and in all He will not disguise Himself or keep you from knowing His will.

There is an enemy that wants to confuse you and mislead you. He is working overtime to keep you from your purpose, but you have a magnificent God who is leading you.

Day 4 Focus Prayer

O Lord, how excellent is your name, how majestic is your power. I submit myself unto you. I pray for total healing for my mind, will and emotions. Give me clarity for my situation. I am overwhelmed by my circumstance and need your divine direction. I cannot do this alone. Set me on my path to victory in Jesus's Name.

Go to your quiet place, meditate on what you read and pray.

Day 5

Day 5

Read Joshua 1. Pray for the spirit of Courage. Many people want to serve God, but lack the courage to press through. They are distracted by many things. There are so many things that can keep you from courageously serving God's purpose. You could be distracted by the illusion that you will miss out on fun, fame, money, connections or even being recognized.

My dear friend, God can give you more. He can make you relevant and give you the peace and joy in Christ that will make your spirit reject the temporary pleasures of this world.

Day 5 Focus Prayer

Dear Lord, righteous and omnipotent Father. Breathe into me courage to fight the good fight of faith courageously. You have been with me from the beginning of time. You have called me into your purpose and I want to do your will. Help me prevail against the distractions that so easily beset me, and work to make me fail in my calling. I will trust the lead of your Holy Spirit in Jesus' Name. Amen.

Go to your quiet place, meditate on what you read and pray for God to give you the courage to press on for Him.

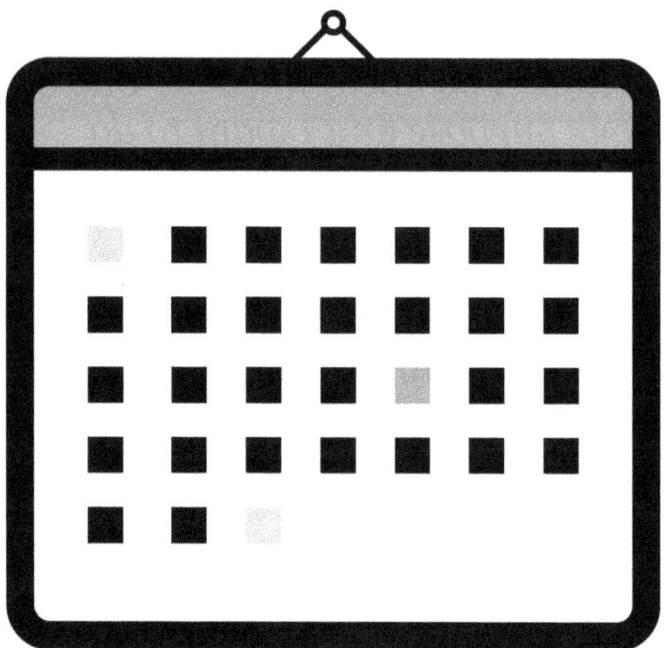

Day 6

Day 6

Read Isaiah 41:10: *"Do not fear, for I am with you; do not be dismayed, for I am your God. I will help you, yes, I will uphold you with My righteous right hand."*

Fear is paralyzing the saints of God, and it has gripped so many people, more than ever before. Fear is keeping so many saints from doing what God has already perfected them to do. Fear will crowd your mind, give you a double-mind and hinder you from your progress in God. If you struggle with fear in spite of having a diligent prayer life, then this is for you.

Go to your quiet place and ask God to help you fully trust Him. You see, the more you see God, the less you will see yourself. The more you trust in God, the less you will trust in yourself. Once your focus is totally on the Lord, everything that once looked like a mountain will begin to downgrade to a valley because it is no longer you facing the challenges, it is Christ!

Day 6 Focus Prayer

I bless your name, O Lord. I give you the glory and the honor. I am so afraid and do not know how to face all of what you have called me to. Help me Lord, as you helped your servant Moses. I feel inadequate to do your will boldly. I need you to fill me up with your holy presence that all I see is you. I will rest in you, in Jesus' Name. Amen.

Go to your quite place, meditate on what you read and pray for God to remove fear from your heart.

Think Outside the Box: 21 Days to A Clear Direction
Prophetess Sebe Dalieh

Day

7

Day 7

Read Romans 8:28: *"And we know that all things work together for good to them that love God, to them who are the called according to His purpose."*

This is your day of New Beginning. On this seventh day, put away everything that once held you back, weighed you down, and caused you to dread. Embrace positivity, adopt positive attitude. I believe that the children of God should walk in the fruit of the Spirit, which is love, joy, peace, long-suffering, gentleness, goodness, faith, meekness, and temperance. When you are walking in the fruit of the Spirit, you exemplify the Christ in you. You have a positive attitude because you know that no matter what happens, God is working on your behalf.

Day 7 Focus Prayer

I will bless the Lord at all times, His praises shall continually be in my mouth. Father, I embrace change, I embrace a positive attitude. I have set my heart upon you. As a deer pants for the waters, so my soul pants for you. I cannot continue doing the same because it has left me broken and out of your will. I am open to receive all of what you have for me in Jesus' Name. Amen.

Go to your quiet place, meditate on what you have read and pray.

Day 8

Day 8

Read Psalm 119:11: *"Thy word have I hid in my heart, that I might not sin against thee."*

It is only the word of God that can give you the clear direction that you seek. I have seen the mighty fall because they chose to walk in their own limited understanding.

Let the word of God be a compass for your life. Set your face like a flint on God's Word. Read it and hide it in your heart so that it can guide you in the right path. God is so much more than we think He is. Humble yourself before Him, walk in meekness, and know that you are nothing without Christ. You were once dead, but now you are alive in Christ Jesus.

Day 8 Focus Prayer

O Lord, you are my peace, you are my joy. I will study your word, hide it in my heart and be obedient unto you. I need to be instructed and guided in your path. I am ready to do all of what you have called me to do. I have made so many mistakes and want to have your peace in my life. Show me your will, O Lord in Jesus' Name. Amen.

Go to your quiet place, meditate on what you have read and pray.

Think Outside the Box: 21 Days to A Clear Direction
Prophetess Sebe Dalieh

Day

9

Day 9

Read Mark 9:23: *"All things are possible to him that believeth."*

Doubt kills so many dreams before they're even started. Doubt kills more dreams than failures. If you struggle with doubt, you hinder yourself from even trying. I will say that it is better to try and fail than to never try at all.

The Lord shall fulfill His good purpose for your life. Be encouraged to renew your hope in Christ. It is not over until God says so. You have to believe in your heart that God is God and that He wants what is best for you. Be just like a child unto the Lord, with unwavering faith. Let Him work on your behalf.

"For truly I say to you, whosoever says to this mountain, 'Be removed and be thrown into the sea,' and

does not doubt in his heart, but believes that what he says will come to pass, he will have what he says." Mark 11:23

Day 9 Focus Prayer

Father, be it done unto me according to your will. I have had doubt in my heart about so many things. Doubt has kept me from doing what I know I should be doing. Doubt has kept me in disobedience and out of fellowship with you. Today, I am replacing my doubt with faith in Christ. I have victory over doubt. I will sharpen my ear in the word of God. My faith comes by hearing the word of God in Jesus' Name. Amen.

Go to your quiet place. Meditate on what you have read, and pray for God's deliverance.

Think Outside the Box: 21 Days to A Clear Direction
Prophetess Sebe Dalieh

Day 10

Day 10

Read Psalm 5:1-14: *"Give ear to my words, O Lord, consider my meditation. Hearken unto the voice of my cry, my King, and my God: for unto thee will I pray. My voice shalt thou hear in the morning, O Lord; in the morning will I direct my prayer unto thee, and will look up. For thou art not a God that hath pleasure in wickedness: neither shall evil dwell with thee. The foolish shall not stand in thy sight: thou hatest all workers of iniquity. Thou shalt destroy them that speak leasing: the Lord will abhor the bloody and deceitful man. But as for me, I will come into thy house in the multitude of thy mercy: and in thy fear will I worship toward thy holy temple. Lead me, O Lord, in thy righteousness because of mine enemies; make thy way straight before my face. For there is no faithfulness in their mouth; their inward part is filled with wickedness; their throat is an open sepulchre; they flatter with their tongue. Destroy thou them, O God; let them fall by their own counsels; cast them out in the multitude of their transgressions; for they have rebelled against thee. But let all those that put their trust in thee rejoice: let them ever shout for joy, because thou defendest them: let them also that love thy name be joyful in thee. For thou, Lord, wilt bless the righteous; with favour wilt thou compass him as with a shield."*

Ask God to give His ear to your prayer. Ask Him to consider you, ask Him to lead you in the direction that He sees fit for you. Surrender all unto Him. Remember that during these 21 days you are seeking a clear direction. Therefore, what you want may not necessarily be what God wants for you. Your wants and desires may be toxic. Ask God to renew your mind so that what you want is what God wants for you.

Wholeness comes when we embrace God's plan for us. Walk in the supernatural - God's *specific* grace, not grace in general. You want God's best, His *Divine* plan, not His permissive plan.

Day 10 Focus Prayer

O Lord, I am casting all of my cares upon you because you care for me. I have so much on my mind. I cannot understand why my choices leave me disappointed and saddened. I need a supernatural turn around.

Hear me O Lord, give me a revelation, show me what to do. I cannot do this on my own. I will wait upon you, O Lord. I will be of good courage and I know You will strengthen my heart. In Jesus' Name. Amen.

Go to your quiet place, meditate on what you have read and pray.

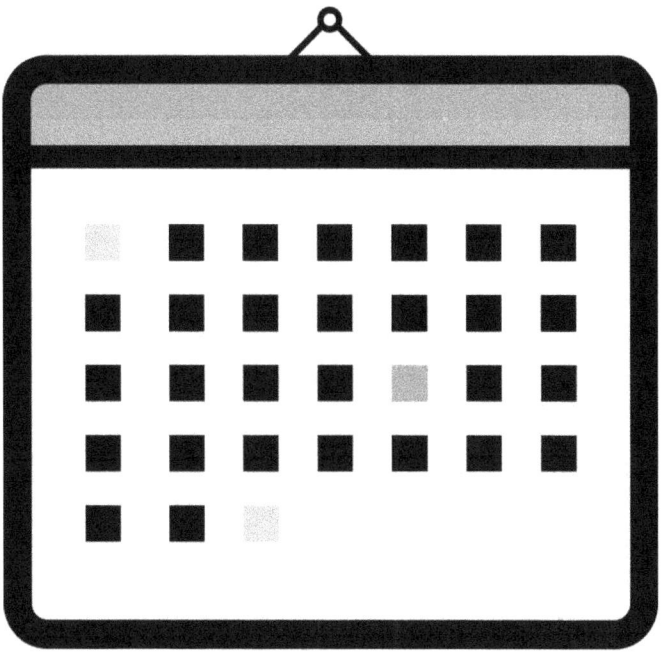

Day 11

Day 11

Read 1 Samuel 30, with particular attention to verse 8. It reads, *"And David enquired at the Lord, saying, Shall I pursue after this troop? Shall I overtake them? And [God] answered him, Pursue: for thou shalt surely overtake them, and without fail recover all."*

In order to get a clear direction, you must pursue God. Inquire of Him. That is what David did in 1 Samuel 30. David was in great distress, after the Amalekites raided Ziklag. He was greatly troubled, and had nowhere to turn. So he inquired of the Lord. Saying, *"Shall I pursue after this troop? Shall I overtake them? And the Lord answered David, pursue: for thou shalt surely overtake them, and without fail recover all."* Samuel 30:8

You must get people out of your ear. Silence your critics, your naysayers, and your agitators. They did not call you, nor did they send you. Therefore, be prepared for them to misunderstand you because God did not give them your vision. Hear one voice and one voice alone. Only one voice should resonate with you, and that voice is the voice of the Lord!

Put to silence every voice that does not align with God's Word or what God is saying to you.

Inquire of the Lord. Know what God says and do what God says.

Day 11 Focus Prayer

O Lord, I will follow after you. Give me a clear direction during this time of prayer. Let me do your will. Let me acknowledge you in all of my ways. Direct my path O

Heavenly Father, to you be all the glory and honor in Jesus' Name. Amen.

Go to your quiet place, meditate on what you have read and God's goodness and pray.

Day 12

Day 12

Read Proverbs 18:21: *"Death and life are in the power of the tongue, and those who love it will eat its fruits."*

I also want you to read James 3:5: *"Even so the tongue is a little member, and boasteth great things."*

The word "tongue" represents your words. Your words have power to sow discord, wound others and even yourself. If you hear or say enough "I Can'ts" there is a possibility that you will start thinking or acting like you "can't". Your words have so much power. Make sure you are not confessing anything that you do not want to have. For you will have what you say.

Your mouth is a pen of a ready writer. You are that writer. Write good words that are aligned with God's purpose!

Pray that the Lord helps you align your thoughts and words according to His word.

Day 12 Focus Prayer

Father, in the name of Jesus, I am empowered to speak words of faith. I am re-aligning my thoughts, words and deeds to reflect you. Your word says as a man thinks in his heart so he becomes. Today, I declare that I will speak only faith words. I believe what God says about me in Jesus' Name. Amen.

Go to a quiet place, meditate on what you have read and pray.

Think Outside the Box: 21 Days to A Clear Direction
Prophetess Sebe Dalieh

Day 13

Day 13

Read Hebrews 10:35: *"Therefore do not throw away your confidence, which will be greatly rewarded."*

Pray for God's confidence. Oftentimes we seek God and receive clarity, but lack the boldness or confidence in God to carry on the call. Confidence is greatly needed because the adversary is out there to accuse you, make you feel unworthy and fill you with guilt. It is your God's confidence that will keep you coming boldly before the throne of grace.

Day 13 Focus Prayer

O Father, my confidence is in you. As I go through this day, I will keep my mind stayed on you. I will walk in total peace as you perfect all of the things that concern me, in Jesus' Name. Amen

Go to your secret quiet place, meditate on what you have read and pray the word of God.

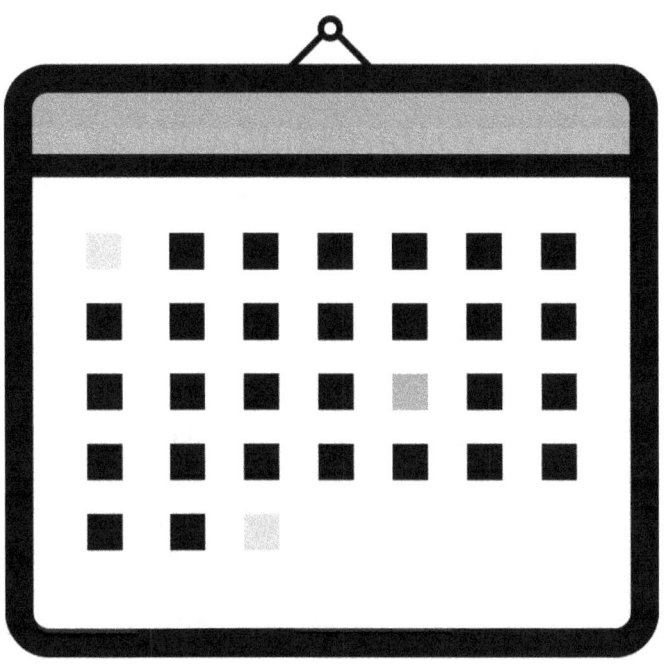

Day 14

Day 14

You are two thirds into your 21 days prayer and meditation. At this time, I want to ask you:

How is your prayer life?

If your prayer life is not strong, I want to encourage you to ask the Lord to teach you how to pray. It is necessary because this is the way you are going to be talking to God and listening to Him. When you pray, make your requests known unto the Lord. Yes, He already knows the requests, but speaking it is for you to affirm what's in your mind. After affirming your thoughts, quiet yourself before the Lord. Once you have quieted yourself, you can hear what God has to say... and sometimes His answer is wait or not yet.

Read Matthew 6:5-13: *"And when thou prayest, thou shalt not be as* the hypocrites are: for they love to pray standing in the synagogues and in the corners of the streets, that they may be seen of men. Verily I say unto you, They have their reward. But thou, when thou prayest, enter into thy closet, and when thou hast shut thy door, pray to thy Father which is in secret; and thy Father which seeth in secret shall reward thee openly. But when ye pray, use not vain repetitions, as the heathen do: for they think that they shall be heard for their much speaking. Be not ye therefore like unto them: for your Father knoweth what things ye have need of, before ye ask him.

"After this manner therefore pray ye:

Our Father which art in heaven, Hallowed be thy name. Thy kingdom come, Thy will be done in earth, as it is in heaven. Give us this day our daily bread. And *forgive us our debts, as we forgive our debtors. And lead us not into temptation, but deliver us from evil: For thine is the kingdom, and the power, and the glory, forever. Amen."*

Day 14 Focus Prayer

Go to a quiet place, meditate, and pray. First, acknowledge God for who He is, give Him thanks, praises, and adoration because He knows it all before you even ask. Father, I thank you! Thank you, Lord because you are thinking about me and before I even was, You were. I celebrated you, O Lord. Second, ask Him for forgiveness, because we are not worthy before Him. It is by His grace that we can come unto Him. Then, tell Him all about the things that concern you.

Day 15

Day 15

Read Psalm 139:

You have searched me, LORD, and you know me. You know when I sit and when I rise; you perceive my thoughts from afar. You discern my going out and my lying down; you are familiar with all my ways. Before a word is on my tongue you, LORD, know it completely. You hem me in behind and before, and you lay your hand upon me. Such knowledge is too wonderful for me, too lofty for me to attain. Where can I go from your Spirit? Where can I flee from your presence? If I go up to the heavens, you are there; if I make my bed in the depths, you are there. If I rise on the wings of the dawn, if I settle on the far side of the sea, even there your hand will guide me, your right hand will hold me fast. If I say, "Surely the darkness will hide me and the light become night around me," even the darkness will not be dark to you; the night will shine like the day, for darkness is as light to you. For you created my inmost being; you knit me together in my mother's womb. I praise you because I am fearfully and wonderfully made; your works are wonderful, I know that full well. My frame was not hidden from you when I was made in the secret place, when I was woven together in the depths of the earth. Your eyes saw my unformed body; all the days ordained for me were written in your book before one of them came to be. How precious to me are your thoughts, God! How vast is the sum of them! Were I to count them, they would outnumber the grains of sand— when I awake, I am still with you. If only you, God, would slay the wicked! Away from me, you who are bloodthirsty! They speak of you with evil intent; your adversaries misuse your name.

Do I not hate those who hate you, LORD, and abhor those who are in rebellion against you? I have nothing but hatred for them; I count them my enemies. Search me, God, and know my heart; test me and know my anxious thoughts. See if there is any offensive way in me, and lead me in the way everlasting.

Pray for whatever your situation may be, whatever it is that is bothering you. Be it your relationship, family, job, finances, or health, pray on what is on your mind and heart. God is listening. Ask God to search you and rid you of the things that are holding you back and bringing damnation into your life.

A word of caution: sometimes these types of prayers can lead to the loss of close family members and friends. You start losing things that meant so much to you, but God sees it differently. He is answering your prayers and ridding you of the things that hinder you.

If you are battling bitterness, resentment, un-forgiveness or anything that you know that is keeping you from progressing in God – put it on the table. God will not only talk to you about other people's faults, He will also show you your own... and what to do to mend them.

Day 15 Focus Prayer

Search me O God and know me. Show me and know my anxious thoughts. Show me the things that are displeasing to you. You know all about me and see my faults from afar. You are the master of discernment. I want to be righteous before you, O Father. Have mercy upon me and be gracious to me, in Jesus' Name. Amen.

Go to your secret quiet place, meditate on what you have read and pray the word of God.

Day 16

Day 16

Read Ephesians 6:10-20: *"Finally, my brethren, be strong in the Lord, and in the power of his might. Put on the whole armor of God, that ye may be able to stand against the wiles of the devil. For we wrestle not against flesh and blood, but against principalities, against powers, against the rulers of the darkness of this world, against spiritual wickedness in high places.*

Wherefore take unto you the whole armor of God, that ye may be able to withstand in the evil day, and having done all, to stand. Stand therefore, having your loins girt about with truth, and having on the breastplate of righteousness; and your feet shod with the preparation of the gospel of peace; above all, taking the shield of faith, wherewith ye shall be able to quench all the fiery darts of the wicked. And take the helmet of salvation, and the sword of the Spirit, which is the word of God: Praying always with all prayer and supplication in the Spirit, and watching thereunto with all perseverance and supplication for all saints; And for me, that utterance may be given unto me, that I may open my mouth boldly, to make known the mystery of the gospel, For which I am an ambassador in bonds: that therein I may speak boldly, as I ought to speak.

Make no mistakes. Now that you have decided to seek the Lord, the enemy will bring attacks in every way, shape and form. You have just entered into warfare. You have to be ready because some things will be purposefully withheld by the hand of the enemy to distract you. But be of good cheer because Master Jesus has overcome it all!

Day 16 Focus Prayer

Re-read Ephesians 6 above so you may learn all about spiritual wickedness and how to guard yourself against it in the word of God.

Go to your quiet place, meditate on the scripture and continue talking to the Lord.

Day 17

Day 17

Read James 1:2-8. Pray for patience. You will need to employ patience because God sometimes will not speak when you want Him to. *"But let patience have her perfect work, that ye may be perfect and entire, wanting nothing."* James 1:4

Therefore, you have to continue to be diligent in seeking Him. He says, *"I will reward them who seek after me diligently."* Hebrews 11:6

Remember, seeking God is not a sprint, it is a marathon. It requires a full lifestyle change that includes training (constant prayer), nutrition (constant study of the Word), and rest (waiting for God's response).

Why does God make us wait? Why must we exercise patience?

Patience is required because God may not come when you want but He is always on time. *His* timing is perfect.

You need to wait on the Lord because His timing is always perfect. Remember, everything that comes in haste is not always good. Wait on the Lord, He will never disappoint you.

Day 17 Focused Prayer

O Lord may I quiet my soul to wait on you, for you know all things. Your will is what's best for me. My hope is built in you, O merciful Father. I will courageously wait upon you, O Lord, in Jesus' Name. Amen.

Go to your quiet place and meditate on what you have read and pray.

Think Outside the Box: 21 Days to A Clear Direction
Prophetess Sebe Dalieh

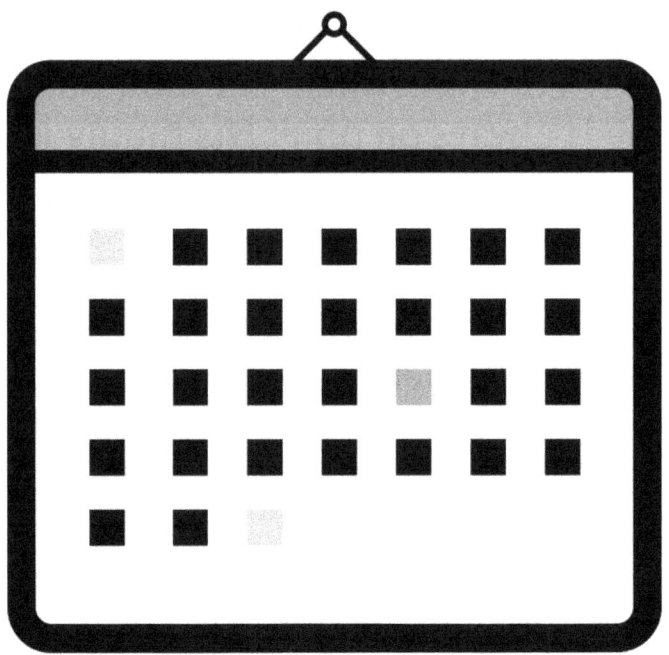

Day 18

Day 18

Read Proverbs 4:7: *"Wisdom is the principle thing; therefore get wisdom: and with all thy getting get understanding."*

Pray for wisdom and understanding. Many times people confuse doing the right thing with doing the wise thing. The right thing to do may not necessarily be the wise thing to do.

For example, someone did something wrong in public. It is *right* to show or tell him/her about the wrong on the spot, but it would be *wise* to show or tell him/her about it in private.

Wisdom and understanding are imperative in walking with God so we do not go before Him and take matters in our own hands that become displeasing to him.

Day 18 Focus Prayer

Lord, I pray that you give me Divine Wisdom and understanding to navigate life. Let your understanding and wisdom be in me. As I study your word, I will take heed to do the things that please you. Holy Spirit, I need your guidance. Instruct me and teach me in the way that I should go, in Jesus' Name. Amen.

Go to your quiet place, meditate on what you have read and pray your focus prayer.

Think Outside the Box: 21 Days to A Clear Direction
Prophetess Sebe Dalieh

Day 19

Day 19

Read Psalm 103. Pray the prayer of thanksgiving unto the Lord. Sing, sing melodies unto Him for He is good and His mercy endures forever. Now say it: *"Bless the Lord, O my soul, and all that is within me, bless his holy name. Bless the Lord, O my soul and forget not His benefits, who forgives all your iniquities, who heal all your diseases, who redeems your life from the pit, who crowns you with loving kindness and tender mercies."* Psalm 103:1-4

Give thanks unto the Lord because He is working on your behalf. He is adding daily blessings to your life. God is getting ready to satisfy your mouth with laughter.

Day 19 Focus Prayer

Lord, I thank you. I praise you for all that I have. I thank you because you are working on my situations. You are perfecting all of what concerns me. I am grateful for my life, my family, my children, my job and all of what you have added to my life and made me manager over. Thank you, O Lord because you are in control of all things and are working to elevate me.

Go to your quiet place and continue to thank the Lord for what He is doing even if you cannot see it. Do it in faith and see it with your spiritual eyes.

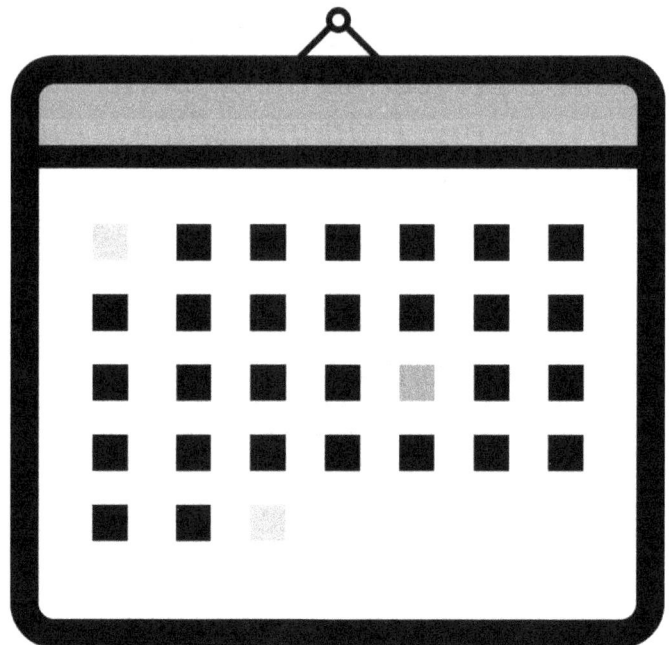

Day 20

Day 20

Read Mark 11:22: "Have faith in God." You are almost at the end of your 21 days. Pray that you do not waiver in your faith. Stand fast in the Lord. He will make good of everything that He has promised. Trust in His word and hold on to His promises. Hold on to the Lord and only the Lord. He is the only one that will never fail you. People will come and go, but God and His word remain forever.

Romans 10:17: "So then faith cometh by hearing, and hearing by the word of God."

At this time, although you are almost done with your prayer and meditation for a clear direction, you still need to be in the Word, reading, studying and listening to God.

Go to church and listen to sermons. You will constantly need to feed your spirit and fuel your faith. Faith comes by hearing - hearing the Word of God. It is by your faith that will bring about what God is saying and doing in your life.

Day 20 Focus Prayer

Lord, I pray that my faith is increased in you. I sealed my faith in the blood of Jesus. I will walk in faith to accomplish God's will for my life, in Jesus' Name. Amen

Go to your quiet place, meditate, pray and listen to what God is saying.

Day 21

Day 21

Read Psalm 46:

God is our refuge and strength, a very present[b] help in trouble. Therefore we will not fear though the earth gives way, though the mountains be moved into the heart of the sea, though its waters roar and foam, though the mountains tremble at its swelling. There is a river whose streams make glad the city of God, the holy habitation of the Most High. God is in the midst of her; she shall not be moved; God will help her when morning dawns. The nations rage, the kingdoms totter; he utters his voice, the earth melts. The Lord of hosts is with us; the God of Jacob is our fortress. Come, behold the works of the Lord, how he has brought desolations on the earth. He makes wars cease to the end of the earth; he breaks the bow and

shatters the spear; he burns the chariots with fire. "Be still, and know that I am God. I will be exalted among the nations, I will be exalted in the earth!"
The Lord of hosts is with us; the God of Jacob is our fortress.

Be still before God in your doings. Do not make any changes unless you are absolutely sure and certain that it is the will of God. Do not change your job, church, family relationships, situation, or marital status. Do not make any permanent change in your temporary situation until you know with absolute certainty it is the will of God. Your situation, no matter what it is, is temporary now that you have made Christ Lord of your life.

Day 21 Focus Prayer

Lord, I have given you all. All of the things that concern me. Take charge of my life. I want to hear from you, O Lord. If I do not hear from you, I will not go on. Show me the way, I pray, O Lord. Show me.

With this prayer, I touch and agree with you that God will meet you right where you are and show you His glory and salvation, In Jesus' Name. Amen.

Conclusion

As you have spent this quality focus time in prayer with the Lord, you are now charged to let the Holy Spirit rule your life and lead you.

You are on the move to be Spirit-Led. Be slow to speak and quick to listen. The Spirit of truth will direct your path. Your steps are now being ordered. You are no longer allowed to make any decisions without seeking insight first, from the Lord. The Holy Spirit will instruct and quicken you in the way that you should go. You are now clothed with the peace of God to operate in His strength. The enemy will fight against you, but he shall not prevail.

My love and peace to you!

About the Author

Sebe Dalieh - The Prophetic Voice, serving God's people around the globe.

This Bible instructor, life coach and confidence booster makes the Bible easy to understand. She's loving, kind and approachable. She loves to see others winning in all walks of life and fulfilling their purpose in God!

Can't find the courage to carry on? Let Prophetess Dalieh energize you with God's Word!

www.ingramcontent.com/pod-product-compliance
Lightning Source LLC
Chambersburg PA
CBHW071121090426
42736CB00012B/1969